T5-DHC-771

Strickland Safari

Jerald D. Johnson is a general superintendent in the Church of the Nazarene.

Upon graduation from Northwest Nazarene College, he pastored several churches in the United States. He and his family then accepted the challenge of opening the work of the Church of the Nazarene in Germany. Following this tenure, he served seven years as executive director of the Department of World Mission, before being elected as general superintendent in 1980. On the Board of General Superintendents, he served as a colleague with Dr. Charles H. Strickland from 1980 to 1988.

Carol Zurcher is the wife of Rev. Norman Zurcher, field director of the Africa South Field. The Zurchers have given 34 years of missionary service to countries in southern Africa.

During simultaneous years of ministry in Africa, the Zurchers shared many experiences of friendship with the Charles Stricklands.

Carol is the author/compiler of three prior NWMS reading books: *Open-heart Sharing with Missionary Wives* (1982), *Rosa: Her Journey of Faith* (1985), and *Memories of Miracles in Africa* (1989).

Strickland Safari

A Legacy of
Commitment and Service

JERALD D. JOHNSON
and
CAROL ZURCHER

Nazarene Publishing House
Kansas City, Missouri

Copyright 1993
by Nazarene Publishing House

ISBN: 083-411-4666

Printed in the
United States of America

Cover Design: Crandall Vail

10   9   8   7   6   5   4   3   2   1

CONTENTS

PREFACE

At the time of his passing, Dr. Charles H. Strickland was serving as general superintendent of the Church of the Nazarene. His jurisdiction was the continent of Africa. He passed away August 9, 1988. He was scheduled to retire 10 months later at the June 1989 General Assembly of the church. At that time, subject to my own reelection, I was in line to assume the African jurisdictional assignment.

Because of his unexpected passing, the Board of General Superintendents decided not to call for a special election but rather to wait and let the General Assembly make the selection. I was requested by my colleagues to assume the Africa responsibilities as well as the ones I already had at that time on the Asia-Pacific Region. This change was made with the assumption that I would continue in Africa for a full two-year term until September 1991. Instead, then, of just a two-year jurisdiction in Africa, I have been privileged to have had nearly three years. This has resulted in several trips to this great continent. And yes, it has included a safari.

I soon learned that wherever I traveled, particularly in the southern regions, I encountered people who freely and affectionately spoke of the Stricklands. Personal experiences were obviously still fresh in their memories. They were still recalling incidents from the time the Stricklands lived in Africa, from 1948 to 1965.

Now I could understand the enthusiasm and love for Africa so frequently and so generously expressed by Dr. and Mrs. Strickland. Obviously their return trips during his last overseas jurisdictional assignment had been especially enjoyable to both of them. His reports to the other members of the Board of General Superintendents, both verbal and written, reflected this.

One man in particular, a brother who has served the African church for a number of years as one of its district superintendents, summarized in one succinct sentence why Dr. Strickland had made such an impact on him. He probably spoke for many different races there. "You see," he said, "Dr. Strickland was the first white man who let me in through his front door."

Two things about Charles Strickland stand out in my mind. One is the obvious lasting impression he made on the lives of many people in Africa. It has left a positive influence on our church there.

The other has to do with my own personal feelings toward this man of God and the fond memories I have of him. After sitting with him for eight years around the general superintendents' conference table, listening to his counsel, hearing him pray, and observing his tears of concern and compassion, I have come to realize he has indeed left a holy influence that has helped mark my own path for service and ministry.

These two conclusions that I have found myself making about Charles Strickland have compelled me to want to share with others his story as I have come to know it. Because our people are a reading people and because Nazarene Publishing House has such a great delivery system for providing literature, it seems logical to use this process for conveying the message. Consequently, many thanks are due Dr. Robert Foster, manager of Nazarene Publishing House, and also Dr. Paul Skiles, Communications Division director, for encouraging and supporting this venture.

Charles Strickland's story really covers two continents—Africa and North America. In order to provide a proper balance, it became apparent that this safari needed to be documented from both areas.

My own time and resources to cover the African side would be limited. It seemed wiser to have someone who lived there research and write for that phase of Dr. Strickland's ministry. Carol Zurcher and her husband, Norman, know the Stricklands, thus enabling her to write with the same personal interest in the story as I. Carol has established her own reputation as a writer, with several of her personal projects accepted for publication. She agreed to cover the African phase of the safari and I the American side of it. She is responsible for chapters 4 through 9. We have endeavored, however, to intertwine the story in such a way as to keep the change in style from being distracting.

Carol is adept at word processing. I'm prone to lumber along with yellow legal pads and handwritten copy. Therefore, I must add the name of Mary Ann Wagner who is deserving of special thanks for her willingness to decipher my handwriting and then transfer it to the modern miracle of word processing machines.

We could never have put the safari together without the help of Mrs. Strickland and her boys. Unexpectedly and suddenly, the Stricklands' oldest son, who was affectionately called "Buddy," died of a heart attack shortly after his father's passing. He was serving as pastor of the Santa Rosa, Calif., Church of the Nazarene at the time. How significant that we were able to retrieve the tribute given to his father before Buddy's own death. Then there were the many others who shared anecdotes and memories with us. All of this combined to reveal a man of sterling character who led a colorful and fascinating life. The title *Strickland Safari* quickly emerged as a natural, for the story is of an interesting and exciting adventure from beginning to end.

You may want to don your imaginary pith helmet, hang a camera around your neck, and prepare to enjoy the safari with us. We invite you to do so and trust you'll enjoy the adventure.

—JERALD D. JOHNSON

SOUTH AFRICA
AND
SWAZILAND

1

WHERE IT ALL STARTED

This is a "safari," a journey full of adventure and excitement. It's the story of a preacher, a great preacher named Charles Henry Strickland. He was born in Cincinnati, Ohio, on October 2, 1916, the only child of his father's second wife, Mary.

Although her parents had raised their daughter in the Roman Catholic church, there were those who became a part of Mary's social circle who influenced her to give her heart to Christ. She worshiped in the Methodist church with these friends who then encouraged her to attend Asbury College in Wilmore, Ky. She graduated with credentials to become a schoolteacher. When she took her first teaching assignment in Atlanta, she became acquainted with Charles Strickland, Sr., and agreed to marry the widower.

Although her new husband did not share her spiritual values, Mary remained true to the influences that she had experienced both in the Methodist church and in Asbury College. Actually, the young wife was very spiritually inclined while her husband refused to attend church with her. After the birth of baby Charles, Mary determined to raise her son in a Christian atmosphere. This became extremely difficult to do, for the father drifted into alcoholism. Charles never did enjoy the normal relationship with his father that he keenly desired. His mother, however, continued to provide strong emotional support, which helped to compensate for that which the father could not give.

Things became so bad that Mary Strickland had no alternative but to commit her husband to an alcohol recovery program. The treatment lasted a full year, a year that proved to be one of tremendous spiritual significance for the son.

At this time they were living in Waycross, Ga. They had been attracted to a small Church of the Nazarene in the community. A pioneer preacher by the name of Roby was the pastor. Mother and son attended services regularly during this period of the father's absence. There was, however, a transportation problem when it came to getting to church. Charles solved it in a unique manner. He had a bicycle, to which he attached a little cushion on the handlebars for his mother. In this manner Charles took the two of them to church regularly.

During this year of the father's absence, the little Waycross church arranged for an evangelist to come for special services. The revival campaign was conducted by an evangelist name Earle Vennum. During these services God spoke to the hearts of both mother and son. They both went to the altar. The mother sought a restoration of her relationship with the Lord. The difficulties of the intervening years since she had left college and entered into marriage had taken their toll, although she had kept her spiritual goals and values intact. This became a great time of genuine revival for Mary. For Charles it proved to be a major religious experience. Later he would date his personal conversion to Christ to this revival campaign in the little church in Waycross, Ga.

When the father returned from his year in the alcohol recovery program, he did not fall in line with his wife and son as one might have assumed. He didn't really oppose Charles and his mother; he just didn't support them. He found it difficult to accept the obvious spiritual development in his son's life. Furthermore, because of the father's limitations due to his own personal problems, the burden of providing much of the financial support for survival rested on the boy, Charles. Again it was the bicycle that helped meet the need.

At 14 years of age, Charles became a Western Union messenger boy. There are those who will recall when teenage lads wearing billed caps with the words "Western Union" written across the tops were a familiar sight in American towns and cities. They always made their deliveries on bicycles. This unique employment helped the family survive during economically hard times.

Being a Western Union messenger boy helped Charles and his mother especially during a time of national crisis. It was 1929 and word of the now-famous stock market crash began to come in over the telegraph wires. This event marked the beginning of the devastating Depression of the 1930s. In the office where he received the messages to deliver, Charles suddenly became aware of the impact that this catastrophe would have on everyone, including the Strickland family. The 14-year-old boy needed no stock-broker to advise him what to do. He simply did what needed to be done and hurried to the bank to withdraw what meager savings he and his mother had accumulated. The wisdom of his decision would never be challenged.

It was hoped that the father's return after his absence of a year would lift the financial burden for the family. However, the elder Strickland apparently was unable to work again. He did receive a pension, but it was very small and grossly inadequate. Western Union and its 14-year-old, industrious messenger boy helped the family survive.

The next two years found Charles and his mother attending church regularly. During this period two preachers had a profound influence on the young teenager. One was J. B. Chapman, who later became a general superintendent in the Church of the Nazarene. Dr. Chapman held a revival in the little Waycross church, and Charles enjoyed him immensely. The other minister, who became his personal friend, was Rev. P. P. Belew. Rev. Belew was superintendent of the Georgia District at that time. This man became acutely aware of the promise in young Charles and often referred to him as his "boy."

There was a third minister who had a profound influence on the young life of Charles Strickland. In retrospect it would appear that God allowed several men to come into his life who would fill the vacuum left by a father who displayed no interest in his son's spiritual development. This third influence was his own pastor at the Waycross church. Charles and his mother had become very active members. Charles had been elected president of the young people's group, a position that kept him in touch with the pastor. They developed a very fine relationship.

The story of an encounter he had with this pastor was so significant to the teenage boy that not only was it a lasting impression on his memory, but it became a turning point in his life.

Shortly before his passing Dr. Strickland found an occasion when it seemed appropriate for him to relate this event in detail. In reading it or hearing it, one is quickly impressed that this did reflect a major turning point in his life and thus deserves special mention in recounting his safari. Fortunately someone with a video camera was present when Dr. Strickland recounted this experience for the last time, just days before his passing. Here is that particular encounter in Dr. Strickland's own words:

We had a pastor when I was a boy who did not have the opportunity of finishing college. He wasn't a well-educated man, and as I remember he made mistakes every now and then in his preaching as far as his English was concerned. But he was a saint of God.

He built a church with his own hands—laid the brick, built it. I helped a little as a boy bringing concrete and mixing it. I remember I helped him build the steps. I thought we'd never get enough concrete to build them.

The day of dedication came. It was a beautiful day, flowers in the church, everything was nice. The district superintendent came; the city officials came. The general superintendent (this dates me, but it was Dr. Goodwin), came to dedicate the building and made a masterful speech.

The pastor got blessed. That didn't bother me because he built the building, and it was time to get blessed about it.

He had the biggest hands I ever saw, and he was clumsy—he was terribly clumsy. He didn't have all the culture that he needed maybe, but in his shouting he got blessed and knocked the flowers over from the table down front. I don't know how in the world he got that far around, but he knocked the flowers over and spilled the water out all over the brand-new carpet.

Now, as I remember that incident—it's been a long time, but—it didn't seem to bother me. He put the stuff down, he could clean it. It was his as far as I was concerned. He built the church. You want to shout, you want to pour water on it—OK.

And I was too young to know, too young to understand. But two or three Sundays later I heard it being talked about at the doors as they were passing by. "Our pastor has built such a lovely church, but he doesn't quite fit the new pulpit. We do need someone now with more education and culture to fit the new building."

I learned what it meant one night in an annual meeting. They voted him out. That was the night that I knew that I had not yet been sanctified, for I became horribly angry. If I could have called fire down, I would have done it. Anybody, any crowd that would let a preacher work that hard and build them a church and then, because he was clumsy, vote him out—I couldn't handle it. My spiritual life wasn't sufficient. I went into the doldrums.

I was NYPS president—the reason being I was the only young person in the church. So we were going to the assembly.

The morning came to travel to the assembly. He pulled the old car out and we went out to the city limits and he stopped.

He said, "Charlie, I went to see the church this morning before I left, walked around it. The bricks are laid well. Before I got all the way around it I had a Visitor. A gentle voice said, 'Son, for whom did you build this church?'" He then said, "Charles, I had to tell Him I built it for Him. I didn't build it for the board; I didn't build it for the people; I built it for Jesus." Then he said, "Come over here a minute."

He put his great big old hands on my shoulders and pulled me up close. I will never forget his prayer. He said, "God, there's a destiny on the head of this young man. But he'll never make it with hate in his heart. Please take it out. Cleanse him, sanctify him, fill him with Your Spirit, and help him to know now and forever that we don't work for a church, we work for God."

Dr. Strickland concluded the story by stating it was on that day he knelt beside that car and there surrendered his life to Jesus, totally and completely. He testified to having received the sanctifying grace of God in his life and heart on that occasion. This proved to be an important preparation for his safari. Many unknowns would be facing him, but the grace that worked for him that day would continue to work throughout a lifetime of service to Christ and His Church.

2

DECISIONS, DECISIONS

The influence of great preachers and a loving pastor, along with a godly mother, helped create an atmosphere in which a very young teenage boy could hear God calling him to be a preacher. His positive response to that call was met, however, with opposition. The father of the lad, who had never looked kindly on the spiritual interest of his son, now expressed open antagonism to his son's decision to be a preacher. Charles let it be known that ministry was his goal and that he would pursue a course that would adequately prepare him. Though this created great conflict between Charles and his father, he never wavered from his goal.

Later, when Charles, Jr., became a pastor, his father relented once and went to hear his son preach. Pride kept him from complimenting his son. But on a later occasion he was heard to say after hearing his son speak, "You know, that son of mine is a [expletive deleted] good preacher."

Charles was convinced his father made it to heaven. He passed away during his son's first pastorate. Charles could not get away to be at his bedside. His mother and a nurse, who happened to be a Christian lady, stayed with the dying man. They were convinced that he had accepted Christ. Although it was a deathbed conversion, there were reasons to believe the repentance was sincere and the conversion genuine. Mary sent a short but very meaningful message to her son. It was a message he would always cherish. It simply said, "Tell Charles he's OK."

During his high school years, Charles' schedule was extremely demanding. After attending school, he would work for Western Union and deliver messages until his route was finished. Then he would go home and work on his homework and study. He rose each morning at six to begin the routine over again. The demands he placed on himself kept him on the high school honor roll.

This industrious spirit would identify Charles Strickland throughout his lifetime. He actually pastored a church at the age of 14. Each weekend he would ride the train 35 miles to the little town of Valdosta, Ga., and then make the return trip. He preached there twice each Sunday. There were times when he could not afford the train. He still made the Sunday appointment by riding his bicycle 35 miles each way.

When he was 16 years old he began to conduct revival campaigns. He was the preacher while two of his friends, Victor Gray and Joe Cook, were the singers. When he was only 18 years of age, he received an invitation from Nashville First Church of the Nazarene. They invited him to be their evangelist for a young people's revival. The services were held under a large tent pitched near the church. Later Charles would frequently refer to this and other similar experiences for the purpose of encouraging young preachers just starting out. He always felt the church should offer such opportunities to young men who testified to a call to preach. He was forever grateful to Nashville First Church for the confidence placed in him as an 18-year-old.

It was at this time that Charles first became acquainted with Fannie, the girl who eventually became his wife. How they met and how he courted and won her hand is a delightful story of love and romance. Joe Cook, one of the two singers who assisted in the revival, was the boyfriend of one of Fannie's sisters. It was Joe who felt Charles and Fannie should get acquainted with each other. During the time of the Nashville revival, the evangelist was served refreshments in a different home after each evening service.

Joe assumed the responsibility of planning the activity for one of the evenings. He approached his girlfriend's sister, Fannie, and asked if she would entertain Charles one evening after the service. She had a quick response, "A preacher? I don't know how to entertain a preacher."

She agreed, however, and proceeded to prepare with diligence. She lived in Nashville with her parents. Charles and the others were invited to her home for refreshments. Looking back on it, Fannie didn't even see the slightest hint of an ulterior motive on the part of Joe, so naive was she. To her there was nothing more in the plans than simply to find the proper way to entertain a preacher.

Fannie did have some concerns. She wasn't sure she knew how to make conversation with a preacher. She would need help. In her mind she concluded the conversation would have to be of a spiritual nature. She decided it would serve her purpose well to become well-versed in the church periodicals. She gathered up all the old issues of the *Herald of Holiness* she could find. Added to these were copies of the *Other Sheep* (forerunner to *World Mission* magazine). All of these she read diligently. In reflecting back on the anticipation of the evening, Fannie now says, "I was scared to death."

In her home following the service, Charles chose to sit on the couch next to Fannie. She may have been naive in regard to the evening's "setup," but Charles was hardly ignorant of the arrangements. He failed, however, to reckon with the very proper upbringing of this lovely southern belle.

When Charles sat next to her on the couch, Fannie looked at him, and with icicles dripping off every word, she said, "And who do you think you are?"

Charles rose to the occasion. Up to this point, Fannie had not been to any of the special services. Perhaps these services could keep alive the first encounter, which was suddenly very important to him. He now asked his own question. "Would you come to hear me preach?" he asked. This she could not refuse.

The very next night she attended the service. To this day, Fannie insists that Charles preached like a bishop. She recalls that the service concluded with the altar lined with seekers. Impressed, Fannie invited Charles to her home again. For this visit Fannie asked her mother to bake one of her special pies for the young preacher.

Pies and sermons proved to be a winning combination. Before leaving town Charles asked Fannie if he could write her. Her consent meant that a period of courtship would flourish. The friendship developed, and Charles claimed Fannie to be his girlfriend. Whenever passing through Nashville he went to see her.

He coupled his enrollment as a freshman at Trevecca Nazarene College with a proposal of marriage. She accepted, and plans were set in motion for a wedding. The formal church wedding plans they had in mind, however, were suddenly set aside due to an unexpected development. Charles, Sr., had become ill, and the son was called home immediately. Fannie didn't want him to go alone; she felt she must be with him. All of this brought about a quick decision to forgo plans for a church wedding and have a simple ceremony in Fannie's home. Actually, they decided to get married the very next day so that Fannie could travel to Charles' home with her new husband.

Family members agreed. A nice, hastily planned ceremony took place. The setting was idyllic for such an event. There was the winding staircase, the piano in the parlor, and a minister to perform the ceremony. Fannie came down the staircase to greet her bridegroom while her sister played the piano. Members of Fannie's family and a few friends were all who were present. The mother of the bride prepared a huge dinner, southern style, for all who were there. It was a very happy event. The date was December 17, 1936.

Upon completion of his two-year ministerial course at Trevecca Nazarene College, the young minister and his wife accepted the pastorate of Moultrie, Ga., Church of the Nazarene. After a time of service there, they accepted the invitation to serve Charles' hometown church in Waycross, Ga. Obviously this congregation believed in their own preacher boy enough to want him now to be their spiritual leader. It was while he was in Waycross that Atlanta First Church of the Nazarene considered calling Charles to be their pastor. The district superintendent cautioned the board by reminding them that the Rev. Charles Strickland was only 25 years of age and there were risks involved with such a young man coming to serve such a great church. The board, however, was unanimous in their feelings on the matter, and the superintendent approved the nomination. Charles and Fannie served the Atlanta congregation for three full years.

General Superintendent J. B. Chapman had eyed the young pastor. He saw in him administrative talents that he felt could be used in another area of service. Dr. Chapman had been given responsibility for finding a district superintendent for the Florida District. At that time the district encompassed the entire state of Florida. Today there are four districts in the same geographic area. The travel requirements alone were awesome.

Dr. Chapman appointed Charles Strickland superintendent of the Florida District. At 28 years of age, he became the youngest district superintendent in the Church of the Nazarene. It appears he may hold that record to the present day.

In Florida, Fannie gave birth to their first child named Charles E. but affectionately called Buddy. Eventually this son also became a minister in the Church of the Nazarene. For a number of years Buddy pastored in South Africa where he had met the young lady who became his wife.

While in Florida, Charles frequently tried to take his wife and baby boy with him so that the long absences would not be so keenly felt. The travel demands were taking a toll on the Stricklands' family life. This, of course, was in the days when travel budgets didn't allow for hotels or motels. It was customary and necessary for pastors to keep their superintendent in their homes. Often the accommodations were very limited. There were more times than not that the Stricklands had one bed for the entire family; this was also before the days of king-size or queen-size beds. Mother, father, and baby boy all in one rather small bed does not make for a good night's sleep. The young father concluded he could not expect his family to live such an abnormal life.

He placed a call to his friend General Superintendent Dr. Chapman and asked if he could be relieved of his duties as superintendent. Providentially, at this same time, he received a call from Dallas First Church to come as their pastor. He had greatly missed the pastoral ministry, and to him this was confirmation enough to feel divine approval for the move.

In Dallas their second son, Wayne, was born. This period of their lives turned out to be a very happy time for the Stricklands. Dallas First was a good, strong church. The routine pulpit ministry was especially challenging to Charles. They had two healthy little boys. Likewise, Fannie was very happy in Dallas. The development of a very special friendship with another Nazarene minister and his wife proved to be especially enriching to the lives of the Stricklands.

Rev. Curtis Smith, later to become known in the denomination as founding president of MidAmerica Nazarene College, was pastoring Central Church in Dallas. His wife, Marge, and Charles' wife, Fannie, became especially good friends. It is a friendship that flourishes to the present day. But it wasn't just the ladies, for Charles and Curt also became good friends. Each Monday morning they routinely met on the YMCA handball court. At noon they were joined by their wives and children for a picnic in the park together. The David and Jonathan dimension of their friendship bonded them together in support of one another throughout their careers. Curt Smith passed away before Charles, and in the last months of Curt's life in a nursing home, Charles visited his bedside each time he returned home from an assignment. Charles grieved over his friend's lingering illness and subsequent passing.

But it was while in Dallas, in this time of fulfillment and contentment, that another call from a general superintendent would jolt the Stricklands out of this happy and secure environment. For the next 18 years their lives would be directed on a course that included a missionary challenge. A course that would have a lasting impact on the lives of many people as well as their own.

The call came from General Superintendent Hardy C. Powers. The request was for the Stricklands to consider an assignment in the Republic of South Africa. It was 1948 and Charles, still a young man, was just 32 years of age.

3

THE DOOR IS OPENED

Fannie simply said no to going to Africa. Why would she even consider such a move? Already in their brief marriage they had been uprooted several times. Moving from Tennessee to Georgia to Florida to Texas was enough, let alone to Africa, and southern Africa at that. She couldn't imagine being any further from home than that. All she wanted was to settle down and normalize her life. Furthermore, she decided that no one, let alone a general superintendent, was going to make them move. She told her husband just how she felt. He in turn contacted Dr. Powers, informing him of their decision to remain in Dallas.

On this occasion Fannie did the talking. She didn't ask Charles how he felt about the matter; she simply told him how she felt. Even if he had positive leanings toward such a move, the fact that his wife was so strongly opposed to the idea was enough for him to back off. Thus for him it was a settled matter; they wouldn't consider the possibility and Dr. Powers should look elsewhere for someone to take the assignment.

After he turned down the offer, Charles returned to the routine of pastoring a great church, determined to give no further thought to Africa. The next morning he went to his study to prepare for Sunday. Fannie was fulfilling her duties as housewife in the parsonage looking after the family. After bathing and feeding Wayne, she placed him in his crib for his morning nap. She then slipped off into a corner of the house that had become her special place to be alone. Following her usual morning routine she moved in to the time she always set aside for her morning devotions. She would read from the Bible as she always did and then spend time in prayer alone with the Lord. This period of quiet meditation had come to be very meaningful to her.

Suddenly she felt a presence in the room. It startled her. She looked up to see who it might be but saw no one. Then she recognized that it was the presence of the Lord himself who seemed to be speaking to her. "Fannie, you didn't ask Me if this move to Africa might be My will for your lives."

Audibly she responded, "Please, Lord, forgive me. You are right. I did fail to ask You." She sensed God's presence to be very real, and her heart became greatly troubled. She then said, "Lord, please forgive me."

During that very sacred and very personal encounter she became convinced that the Lord himself was indeed speaking to her. Furthermore, the message she received was that the call to Africa was from Him, not just from a general superintendent. She felt deeply convicted, and she also became sincerely submissive. She was ready to go to Africa. Furthermore, she was ready to go immediately if that seemed the right thing to do.

A great burden lifted; there was joy in her spirit. She even found herself wanting to go to Africa. But, of course, Charles would have to know. She hurried to the telephone and excitedly tried to call him.

Charles had gone to his study that morning to begin preparation for the next Sunday's services. But just as the Lord had spoken to Fannie in the parsonage, He spoke to Charles in the study of the church, apparently at the very same time. Suddenly the pastor felt a great burden of prayer being laid on his heart. He could not get the thought of Africa out of his mind. He concluded that perhaps that burden to pray had come about through the events of the past few days.

In this quiet time he found his mind being challenged as to why the general superintendent had been so intent on finding someone to go to that continent. Charles was aware, as he supposed were all Nazarenes, that the Church of the Nazarene had been in Africa for many years. He knew well the history dating back to the days of Harmon and Lula Schmelzenbach. The stories of their struggles in pioneering the church in southern Africa had never ceased to thrill his soul. He, along with thousands of others, had a rather provincial, stereotyped image of what it means to be a missionary. He had never seen himself in that role.

However, Dr. Powers had presented a completely new and innovative idea; at least it was one Charles had never heard of before. This one would not fall into traditional missionary patterns. In fact, Dr. Powers avoided calling it a missionary project; rather, he chose to call it "overseas home missions."

The assignment was directed toward the Europeans of South Africa. The system of racial separation instilled into South African life did complicate matters as far as the church was concerned. Regardless of how the church leaders felt about the system itself, circumstances would require facing the realities of it if all segments of South African society were to be reached. Before this point in time the white population had not been targeted by the Church of the Nazarene. It was the desire of Dr. Powers to reach them as well and bring them into the church.

In recent years—even months—the world has witnessed the disassembling of apartheid. This has brought welcome relief to the Church of the Nazarene. In many respects the Church of the Nazarene has been ahead of the times in these developments. Part of the assignment for Charles Strickland back in 1948 was to provide communication between those who would be working with various ethnic and language groups.

Back in his study that early morning in Dallas, Charles Strickland tried to put all of these complicating factors in perspective. He found no easy solutions to the puzzling questions that were heavy on his mind.

Before he had returned Dr. Powers' call to say that they would not be going to South Africa, Charles had received some material that would give him some knowledge on the subject. He had read that most of the European people in South Africa were of Dutch descent. These people had brought the Dutch language with them. Over a period of time the Dutch language had been influenced by local languages. The resulting mixture has come to be known as Afrikaans. For anyone to reach Afrikaans-speaking people, this language would have to be studied and learned.

But he had also read about Europeans in South Africa of English descent. Language would really not be a problem, although an American southern dialect might have to be adapted in order to be understood. There would, of course, be necessary cultural adaptations to be made with both groups of Europeans. The request of the general superintendent was to plant churches for both language groups. Surely this in itself would be a challenge: eventually to bring all together under one umbrella as one district.

These became reasons enough for Charles Strickland not to accept the assignment. He had no formal training for such a formidable task. Compounding all of this with the unmistakable reaction of his wife to the call was occasion for him now to dismiss the subject from his mind and to get on with living and serving in Texas.

He walked out of his study into the sanctuary of the church. He sensed a strange tugging that drew him in the direction of the altar. Once he got to the altar he felt further prompted to kneel and pray. Suddenly a great burden for Africa settled upon him. He seemingly could not work his way out from under it. The more he prayed, the heavier the burden became. The intensity of it convinced him that this was God's way of speaking to him. He also knew there was no escaping the conclusion to which he was being drawn. Fannie, Dallas First Church, family—all were placed on the altar; and Charles conceded his willingness to go to Africa.

But he would have to tell Fannie. How could he do so? In his praying he cried out further, "Lord, if You want me to go to Africa, You'll have to convince Fannie." Of course, Charles had no way of knowing what had been taking place in the parsonage. It was at this same time that Fannie jumped up from her knees and ran to the telephone. She called her husband's study. He was still in the sanctuary, contemplating his next steps, when he wondered why the telephone insisted on ringing so persistently. He concluded it was a parish emergency and hurried to answer it.

When he picked up the phone, he heard a woman crying on the other end of the line. He recognized it to be his wife who said to him, "Honey, come home quick. Something has happened."

"Are you hurt?" he asked.

"No."

"Is the baby sick?"

"No."

"Well, what's wrong?"

"The Lord just told me we've got to go to Africa."

Charles hurried home. Excitedly they compared notes with one another. Where there had been anxiety there was now joy. They shared in the anticipation of a new and exciting adventure. They checked the clock; it was 10:30 A.M. They needed to call Dr. Powers to tell him. Then they remembered that they had already called him and turned down the assignment. What if he had already moved on to someone else? How would they reconcile this with what they had both experienced?

When they called Dr. Powers he asked to meet both of them for lunch. Dr. Powers made his home in Dallas and happened to be in at the time. The minutes between

10:30 and noon seemed long and drawn out. In the restaurant they quickly got to the point. Was the offer still standing or had he contacted another? The general superintendent's response reflected his own inner conviction. "No, I haven't," he replied. "You see, I knew all the time that you would take the assignment." A great sense of relief settled down upon Charles and Fannie Strickland. Already in their minds they began to make preparations for the long move to Johannesburg, South Africa.

4

WE'RE GOING TO AFRICA!

As the Pan American Clipper airliner winged its way out over the Atlantic on August 26, 1948, the challenging African leg of the Strickland safari began. The precious human cargo on board were Charles and Fannie and their two sons, six-year-old Charles (Buddy) and 18-month-old Wayne. Left behind, in obedience to God, were loving families, a comfortable home country and customs, and the established home church. A vast unknown land and a variety of peoples, languages, customs, and cultures lay ahead of them.

Nazarene missionary work had started much earlier among the various African peoples in southern Africa. The missionaries and nationals had joined in earnest prayer concerning their mutual burden of the evangelization of their country. They longed to see the Church of the Nazarene preaching holiness among the white people there.

In 1944 the Africa Mission Council had sent a strong resolution to the Department of World Missions urgently requesting that someone be appointed to open this work. When General Superintendent Hardy C. Powers visited the field in 1947, he saw this great need personally. So it was after his trip that he had approached the Stricklands to go to South Africa. They were to go under the Department of Home Missions to establish work with the English-, Afrikaans-, and Portuguese-speaking South Africans, who each have distinct cultures as well as languages.

While still waiting in the States for their residence permits, Charles did some evangelistic work. During this time they met with Dr. W. C. Esselstyn, superintendent of the African work, to talk about the country and the work in southern Africa. During their lunch together in St. Louis, they watched Dr. Esselstyn eat with his fork upside down, as he used his knife in good British and South African fashion. Fannie confessed later that she had whispered to Charles, "Poor old Mr. Esselstyn has been out there in Africa so long he doesn't know how to eat properly any longer!" They wondered what new things they would be learning and if they would seem a bit strange too after living overseas for a while.

Shortly before their departure, Charles was involved in a serious car accident. Although his vehicle was totaled, God spared him from injury. During their flight to Africa, the plane attempted to land in West Africa for refueling. They knew they had nearly landed in dense fog and then zoomed back up into the air. What they did not know was that they had actually been over the ocean and not the runway when the plane had started to descend. God had spared them once again and took them safely to their new assignment.

During the long flight Charles' mind was filled with many questions. How and where would they begin this new work? . . . How would they be received by the people? . . . Would he be able to learn the Afrikaans language? . . . Where would they find preachers? . . . How would they train them? . . . Only assurance of God's clear direction and presence gave him a calmness of spirit that God would provide the answers when they were needed.

The weary but excited Strickland family were met by several missionaries when their plane landed in Johannesburg on August 28, 1948. Fannie disembarked first, holding firmly to curious little Buddy's hand. Charles followed close behind, carrying toddler Wayne in his arms.

As they left the airport they drove through the heart of the great city of Johannesburg, which had a population of 1 million at that time. The Stricklands eagerly viewed the modern buildings, wide streets, bright lights as well as the great variety of peoples. On seeing all of this his earnest comment was, "If prayer and hard work can get the job done, that is all I have to offer." Through the years that followed, Charles Strickland proved beyond doubt that prayer and hard work were the chief cornerstones on which he laid the firm foundation for building the European work of the Church of the Nazarene in southern Africa.

Missionaries Paul and Mae Hetrick had driven the Stricklands to the home of missionaries George and Jeanette Hayse. It was there they spent their first weeks in Africa. Those early days helped orient them to their adopted homeland as they had a variety of new experiences. Charles read 14 books on South Africa in 14 days. They formed a deep appreciation for the dedicated missionaries and their devoted work among the African people.

Several weeks after their arrival, a district parsonage was purchased in Discovery, near Johannesburg. Fannie's affluent southern family had been concerned about their housing and safety in Africa. After moving into their new home, with tongue in cheek, Charles wrote to her family informing them that he had managed to find a simple hut down near the river in which their little family could live. He assured them that although it was a bit primitive he had a shotgun standing near the door to kill any snakes or wild animals that might come near . . . that he was doing his best to protect them. To dispel their mounting fears, he then sent them a photo of their comfortable, modern, brick home in the well-developed suburb.

The two official languages of South Africa are English and Afrikaans, although a number of other languages are also spoken by the various ethnic peoples. Charles was informed before arriving that one of his first tasks would be to study the Afrikaans language in order to minister effectively to the Afrikaans-speaking people. He took double courses in Afrikaans for several months.

One afternoon he was in his study, deeply engrossed in pronouncing some of the more difficult sounds and words of the Afrikaans language. In the midst of this practice session, Fannie suddenly burst into the room and asked if he was sick. After that he would inform her when he was going to be studying out loud so that she wouldn't be alarmed over his state of health.

Eventually his diligent efforts were rewarded and he could converse and preach in the language. His use of their language, although with an American accent, endeared him to the Afrikaans people and helped to reach them for Christ and the church.

Early in their South African safari, Charles was traveling on a commuter train. As he chatted with the people in the compartment, he asked them a variety of questions. In return, someone queried him, "What do you do?"

He said, "I am a minister in the Church of the Nazarene."

When they responded that they had never heard of that church, he exclaimed, "Where have you been all of your life?"

Of course, the Church of the Nazarene was virtually unknown among the white population in the country at that time. But that incident was indicative of the positive attitude with which Charles Strickland tackled this challenging new assignment for God and the Church of the Nazarene.

5

ALL THINGS WORK TOGETHER

Charles earnestly prayed for divine direction concerning how to proceed in starting this new work. He was encouraged by the missionaries and nationals working in the Johannesburg area who had prayed for their appointment.

He pursued every lead where he heard there was interest in a holiness church. There were times when he would be away from home for weeks at a time.

On one occasion, he drove over 300 miles of harsh dirt road to call on one solitary farmer. He spent the night talking to him about the things of the Lord. The following day he returned the same way he had come.

Another time he sat in his car and waited for three days for a swollen river to subside so that he could cross over to see the people he wanted to visit.

Services were conducted in tents, rented halls, and homes in the cities as well as in the country. Often attendance was very small and not all campaigns were fruitful. Charles would preach as earnestly to two people as he would to a large crowd, and God honored His Word. Often the few people who attended would quickly leave as soon as the sermon was completed. Charles finally made a habit of asking Fannie to pray the closing prayer and instructed her to pray long enough so that he could get to the door to meet the people as they left.

They had been in South Africa for several months and progress in the work seemed slow. One day Charles received a letter from General Superintendent Hardy C. Powers inquiring about how the work was progressing and what he was doing.

In his discouragement Charles turned the letter over and wrote "NOTHING" on the back.

He received a prompt reply saying he had not been sent to Africa to do nothing and that he'd better get busy.

He spent more time in sermon preparation than he had planned. During his teens and early years in the pastorate, Charles attended many camp meetings and revivals. He jotted down many sermon outlines and notes from messages he heard that he thought might help him in the future. He had packed them in a box to ship to Africa. When Fannie came across it she thought it was a box of junk and threw it out.

Charles and Fannie were a warmhearted, friendly couple who won the hearts of the people. God blessed his ministry of holiness evangelism. Branch Sunday Schools, house-to-house visitation, and personal soul winning were also keys that reached open hearts.

During those early months the following four definite conclusions were reached from which they did not depart across the years:

1. We must major on holiness evangelism.

2. We must organize the church among both the English- and the Afrikaans-speaking language groups.

3. We must identify the name of our church with all of our activities.

4. The success of our church will depend on the development and training of South African ministers.

The following are some examples of those early meetings:

Soon after their arrival, they were told that the Johannesburg suburb of Kensington was the ideal spot to start the

Church of the Nazarene. They rented a hall there that would seat 300 or 400 people. The meetings were advertised in various media, and many brochures were distributed. The Strickland family arrived early to greet the crowds of people who would respond. Service time arrived and the Rev. Dr. Charles Strickland preached to his wife and two sons, who made up the entire crowd.

After the third Sunday, young Buddy remarked, "Daddy, why don't we find a big bell to ring? Then maybe the people would come!" He remembered that the people had always come to their church in Dallas when they rang the bell.

Teenage M.K. Ted Esselstyn helped in this project and attended the meetings quite regularly with the Stricklands. It amazed him that Dr. Strickland would hold each service and preach fervently, with the tears running down his face, even though most of the time the congregation consisted of just the Strickland family and himself.

Later, after holding services for 10 Sunday evenings, Charles arrived at the hall and removed the sign. When he went inside he found 24 people waiting for the service! He quickly replaced the sign and announced that the services would continue.

* * *

In the industrial town of Vanderbijl Park, a campaign was conducted for a month, and the largest attendance was about 15. Not even one hand was raised for a prayer of salvation. At the close of the meeting, Dr. Strickland organized the church with four members: the Stricklands and the Bothas, the pastor and wife. This later became one of the strongest Afrikaans churches on the district.

* * *

One evening after a service in the small church at Regents Park, Johannesburg, layman Clarrie Roux met Dr. Strickland. For 14 years he had been a member of a holiness crusade in downtown Johannesburg, which no longer had a place to meet. Thrilled to find a denomination that preached the message of holiness, he inquired if the Church of the Nazarene would hold services in central Johannesburg.

Dr. Strickland replied, "Clarrie, you go and find a hall and we will get started." He soon found a hall in the very heart of the city on the second floor for a very nominal rental fee.

Clarrie and a few others, along with Charles Strickland, cleaned up the hall and services were started. Twelve people attended the first service.

They moved to different halls as the congregation rapidly grew. In spite of his many duties in beginning the church across southern Africa, Dr. Strickland pastored this church for over a year.

Many young people were attracted to this new church, and it grew to around 60 members. Even though this group later merged with the Regents Park congregation, it probably was one of the most effective of all the churches in terms of producing full-time workers for the Church of the Nazarene.

* * *

Rain was pouring down one day when Dr. Strickland and Rev. Kosie Coetzee were going into the Kalahari desert to hold special meetings at some isolated farms. They came to a place where they had to cross the river. The water was high, and the river was flowing swiftly over the bridge.

They wondered whether it was safe to pass through. Kosie rolled up his pant legs and waded into the water to see how deep it was and how strong the current was flowing.

Dr. Strickland was frightened and exclaimed, "No, brother, we can't go through!"

But Brother Coetzee insisted, saying in Afrikaans, "No, Dr. Strickland, we must go through! We have a message for tonight!"

They breathed a prayer and made preparations to cross over. Dr. Strickland rolled up his pant legs and waded through the swirling river while Rev. Coetzee slowly and carefully guided the car through.

They kept their appointment, and God blessed their service. This experience made a lasting impact on Dr. Strickland, and he used that story many times later in his sermons as he challenged his listeners, "We must go through!"

* * *

Although there were many discouraging days in the beginning of the work, Charles and Fannie encouraged each other to carry on in the work that God had sent them to do. Often just when they concluded there was no interest, they would suddenly receive an unbelievable response. For the most part, churches were organized from among their own converts as a result of their campaigns and follow-up work.

Missionary Dr. Ted Esselstyn recalls: "After the initial difficult days were over, it seemed as if the work among the Europeans developed very quickly. Every few weeks our family would join the Stricklands for the organization of a new congregation or the dedication of a new church building, or for some other special event in the work. The opening of churches in Southern Rhodesia, Northern Rhodesia, and Mozambique was the cause of great rejoicing.

"Dr. Strickland impressed us not only as a preacher but also as a practical person, for when necessary he set up a workshop in his garage and turned out furniture for the churches. He set up a print shop and turned out literature. He was willing to do whatever was needed in order to get the gospel to the people."

In a letter to missionaries on June 1, 1950, less than two years after their arrival, Charles wrote: "You will be glad to learn that your prayers are being answered. I have just concluded three months of continuous preaching in revival campaigns, and God has answered all of our prayers in a most remarkable way. Within the past three months I have helped to bring 170 people into the experience of salvation or holiness. Three new churches have been established and most remarkable of all, God has provided us with a pastor for each."

The deep spiritual preaching and earnest zeal of Charles Strickland reached the hearts of the South Africans. Men and women who had heard the message of holiness under the ministry of independent preachers now turned to the Church of the Nazarene.

God gave wisdom and guidance as to the men who were selected to pioneer the church in its early beginnings. They came from varied walks of life. Some had strong British traditions. Others had strong Afrikaans backgrounds. Some brought with them a good record of service in the ministry with other groups. Drawing them together was their common zeal concerning the doctrine of holiness. Thus they developed a strong Church of the Nazarene.

By the time the Stricklands had been in South Africa two full years, eight churches had been organized and five preaching missions established with a membership of 160. They had two ordained elders and four licensed ministers working with them.

On October 24, 1950, General Superintendent Powers declared that the new South African District be created with a stroke of his gavel—the same gavel that had been presented to him by the Africa Mission Council in 1947. One lady exclaimed, "The sound of that gavel was surely heard in heaven!" A number of Nazarene missionaries were also present, and all hearts rejoiced together over what God had done. The new district was off to a good start—on the road to self-support. Sunday Schools and young people's societies became a part of the program in each local church.

Fannie started the Nazarene World Missionary Society in each new church. Time and again she explained the detailed organization and procedures. Seeing the increasing interest and vision that these new Nazarenes had for others brought the Stricklands great joy. The district has produced several who have or are currently serving as Nazarene missionaries.

During their 18 years in Africa, the Stricklands saw 29 churches established in South and Central Africa, with most of them thriving yet today.

6

BABIES, BLESSINGS, AND BIBLE COLLEGE

Very early in the development of the new work, the need for a Bible college to train Nazarene ministers became apparent. Charles remembered his phone call to Dr. Hardy C. Powers the night before they left from New York to fly to South Africa. On inquiring if he had any final instructions, Dr. Powers replied simply, "Africa is 9,000 miles away and God is in heaven. You will have to trust God's guidance in the securing and training of ministers in that country."

This urgent need was discussed with Dr. Powers when he was in South Africa for their first assembly in 1950. A commission was elected to study the possibility of a site for the school in 1951. They received the good news that the General Nazarene Young People's Society was going to sponsor a special project to help finance the opening of the college in 1952.

Writing in the May 1952 *District Bulletin,* Dr. Strickland shared: "The preservation and propagation of the doctrine of holiness in experience and practice depend largely upon a God-called, Holy Spirit-illuminated, and properly trained ministry. Where the Church of the Nazarene has gone with the message of holiness the educational need has followed closely upon its evangelism. For many months we have felt the need of a training center in South Africa. We could not do it ourselves. We are part of a world-church which has a vision for spreading the Gospel of Christ to every nation. The Nazarene Young People's Society will take this project and bring us financial assistance to bring a Bible college to South Africa."

During this time in their African safari, Charles and Fannie learned to their joy that Buddy and Wayne were going to have a new little brother or sister. They were especially delighted when they were informed they were going to have twins.

The lone, dark cloud in their sky was the disappointment of the pastors when they learned that Charles would not be able to go to the General Assembly in 1952. It was planned that he would present the project of raising funds to begin the college that was so desperately needed. But he had decided not to travel because of the impending birth of the twins. If he didn't go, this project might be delayed for another four years.

God began to deal with Fannie. She felt certain that Charles must go to the General Assembly and God would take care of her. She realized that the training college for ministers was very urgent for the development of the work.

She had to do a great deal of persuasive talking to convince Charles to leave her and the boys in Africa and return to America for the General Assembly. She calmly reassured him that he would return in time for the birth of the twins.

However, their twin boys, Dudley and Douglas, put in their appearance early, while Charles was still overseas in June of 1952. Fannie experienced a very difficult time following their birth due to kidney poisoning. She went into convulsions and lost her eyesight. A specialist from Johannesburg was called in. This crisis was a time of intense testing on their safari.

Concerned family, friends, and Nazarenes in America prayed. They were joined by missionaries, nationals, and the new Nazarenes in southern Africa. In answer to prayer, God spared Fannie's life. Her vision was restored. God gave them two healthy boys. And South Africa received the money to start the Bible college.

This special offering of $20,000 made possible the purchase of a property adjoining the church in Potchefstroom, 240 kilometers southwest of Johannesburg, for the new Bible college. Thus the church building could be used for chapel and other services. All preliminary plans were made. A constitution was drawn up, and an academic program was prepared. Six ministerial students enrolled in the first class in January 1954. This was a triumphant highlight on the new district.

One of the most difficult problems in operating the Bible college was the language problem. The textbooks were in English, and it sometimes proved to be difficult for the Afrikaans-speaking students. Classes were held in both English and Afrikaans. The students were allowed to write examinations in their home language.

Two or three times a week, Dr. Strickland drove to Potchefstroom to teach classes. This, together with all his other responsibilities on the new district, made him a very busy man.

The first graduation ceremony took place in November 1955. Soon after that Rev. Floyd Perkins was appointed as principal and served as a dedicated, capable leader for 12 years.

In 1962 the college was moved to Florida in the Johannesburg area. A variety of dedicated South Africans have served as principals, lecturers, and staff at the college. It has produced many pastors and several Nazarene missionaries over the years.

Dr. Strickland's life and teaching made a great impact on all who listened to his lectures and ministry during their student years. The following are just a few of the incidents remembered by former students now in the Lord's work:

Pastor's wife Betty van den Berg described Dr. Strickland as a gracious gentleman with a Southern drawl who did not get excited easily. She recalls that he told the students of an incident in the States when he was invited to fill the pulpit of another preacher. This man was very lively and had the reputation of jumping up and down and running around while preaching. He thought he had better do some of the same in order to keep the congregation's interest. So at the right moment, he took off running to the end of the platform.

His preschool son, Buddy, who was seated on the front pew, was so surprised and excited about this unexpected activity that he yelled out, "Do it again, Daddy, do it again!"

In sharing this with his students he encouraged them to always be themselves in the pulpit and not try to imitate others.

* * *

While in Bible college, one of the students was responsible for the services in a nearby town. God blessed his ministry and sermons. On reporting to Dr. Strickland, he asked the student, "Where do you think God finds these sermons you are passing on to your people?" The student replied that he did not know.

He was reminded of the importance of his studies. Through them he was storing knowledge in his mind, stocking the shelves as it were—reading books, praise and worship, and his own private devotions. When it was needed, God slipped a little knowledge off the shelves for him to use. Dr. Strickland added, "If you fail to fill the shelves, you'll not have anything to give or use in return."

* * *

The students who were about to graduate and go out into the ministry had a standing joke.

It seemed that if Dr. Strickland was going to give you an assignment to pastor nearby in the Johannesburg area, he would invite you to his home for tea or a meal. If he took you out to eat, that usually meant that he was going to assign you farther away.

In the case of John and Jean Marks, the Stricklands took them out to a Chinese restaurant to eat and during the evening he asked them to go the great distance to Central Africa to pastor a church!

* * *

Some of the things the students remember him saying include:

"Go where they don't want you, and stay until they can't do without you."

"Don't make decisions in the valley—the valley of discouragement, illness, financial pressure, or any other."

"Treat people as you would have them become—not as they are. Otherwise, they will stay that way."

"Don't seek position; let position seek you."

* * *

A few years after the church in South Africa was established, a young German immigrant, Richard F. Zanner, had his first contact with the Church of the Nazarene in the home of his girlfriend's mother. Mrs. F. Auditore, a strong Christian lady, had opened her home for Bible studies and prayer meetings to the embryo congregation of the Church of the Nazarene at Horizon, near Johannesburg. Richard had come to South Africa with a scholarship to study for engineering in the gold mines.

All efforts to reach this young man with the gospel were rejected for some time. But the patient pastor, Rev. Thomas, continued to show concern and prayed for him, along with his congregation.

Eventually Richard was wonderfully converted. Later on he was sanctified and called into the ministry. He fell in love and married Valerie, that fine young lady in whose mother's home he first met Nazarenes.

Fannie Strickland was in the service the day Richard gave his heart to the Lord and told her husband about it. He had met Richard on two previous occasions and saw great potential in this talented young man.

Richard, at that time branch manager of an insurance company west of Johannesburg, began attending classes at Nazarene Bible College in Potchefstroom. He often rode the many miles from Johannesburg to the college with Dr. Strickland. These were interesting trips. Richard had so many questions about this, that, and the other, that challenging debates about the doctrines of the Church of the Nazarene ensued between them on those trips. Dr. Strickland patiently and lovingly answered Richard's questions.

Late in 1960, Horizon church held a revival campaign in Roodepoort, where a tent was pitched for that purpose. Richard, among others, was very involved during that week, which also gave him opportunity to use his musical talent by playing his accordion for the services. Missionaries Norman and Carol Zurcher were the song evangelists, and Dr. Strickland was the powerful preacher-evangelist.

With this tent campaign in Roodepoort, Richard's time in South Africa (eight years) drew to an end. His father became terminally ill in Germany, and Richard returned home to be at his bedside. He was able to lead him to the Lord before he passed away.

Having felt the burden to help establish the Church of the Nazarene in his own country for some time, Richard considered it a "wink from heaven" when Dr. Jerald D. Johnson, at that time pioneer missionary for the church in Germany, asked him to stay and to help build a district. Valerie and the two children, Ingrid and Cheré, after selling the house and the household in South Africa, followed early in 1961.

Exciting days of pioneering the church in the center of Europe ensued as Richard and Valerie forged a new friendship with Alice and Jerry Johnson in these early days of Nazarene history in Europe.

Richard pastored Frankfurt First Church for 9 years and was then elected first national district superintendent of the Middle European District. They served for 11 years in that assignment. The Zanners returned to South Africa in 1980 when he was appointed first regional director for the church outside of the United States.

God continues to use the early fruits of the outreach of the district and college through the zealous, committed ministry of Richard Zanner and many others who were won to the Lord and the Church of the Nazarene during those days of "testing and triumph."

Rev. Strickland at the Heidelberg printing press (early 1960s)

Rev. and Mrs. Charles H. Strickland, 1964.

Professor Charles H. Strickland at Nazarene Bible College, South Africa (early 1960s).

Dr. and Mrs. Charles Strickland on visit to South Africa as general superintendent, 1986.

Dr. and Mrs. Charles Strickland with Dr. and Mrs. Richard Zanner (director of Africa Region), 1986.

Dr. and Mrs. Strickland with missionaries Norman and Carol Zurcher, 1986

Dr. and Mrs. Strickland, the Zanners, the Zurchers, and ordination group in South Africa, 1986.

Dr. and Mrs. Strickland, Dr. Zanner, and ordination group in Swaziland, 1986

7

HOT OFF THE PRESS

Dr. Strickland was a prince of a preacher. He would be moved to tears very easily while preaching. At first this seemed strange in the conservative, reserved South African culture. His tender spirit, often accompanied by tears, became a trademark of his preaching.

Once a Sunday School teacher was reviewing the different Bible prophets whom she had been studying with her students. She asked who was known as the "weeping prophet." One child eagerly raised his hand and quickly answered, "Dr. Strickland!"

His illustrations were always very descriptive and to the point. Rev. L. J. Kriel remembers when Dr. Strickland was preaching on the necessity for unity and harmony in a congregation in order to be successful. He used the following illustration: There is a difference between unity and harmony. It is harmony that makes the difference in community life. When you tie two cats' tails together, then hang them on a washline, you have unity, but you have no harmony.

The following bear testimony of Dr. Strickland's powerful and far-reaching ministry:

As a young couple, Gideon and Jeanette Tredoux had heard the message of full salvation. Having experienced the cleansing power of Jesus' blood, they were looking for a church that preached the doctrine of holiness.

In 1958 someone invited them to go hear an American preacher at the Church of the Nazarene. They had never heard of that church and thought it was just another sect that had come from America. Gideon was hesitant to attend the meetings, but Jeanette thought they should at least find out what that church believed.

The last night of the meeting they went together to the service, which was held in the sitting room of the only member. There were just a few people present, but Dr. Strickland preached the Word with great power as if there were a big crowd present. It seemed to them as if his booming voice would lift the roof off the building. To their great surprise, Gideon and Jeanette discovered that the Church of the Nazarene preached what they already experienced. They felt this was the church they would like to join . . . and they did.

Today they are Nazarene missionaries serving in Malawi.

* * *

Missionary Jaap Kanis tells of Dr. Strickland's preaching: "The power punches in his preaching were the illustrations, especially the ones he used to close his sermons. Many times they came from his own experience. They were genuine and the Lord used them. He relived them while they were related and usually took his audience with him. It was never difficult for a person to go to the altar after Dr. Strickland preached."

* * *

What Salom Dlamini from Swaziland has always remembered about Dr. Strickland is a message he preached one time in Manzini. He was asked to speak at a graduation service for student teachers. He used John 12:24 as his text, "Verily, verily, I say unto you, Except a corn of wheat fall into the ground and die, it abideth alone: but if it die, it bringeth forth much fruit."

One statement he made has meant a lot to her down through the years. He said, "What you are means more than what you know. You may have the knowledge, but your real self is more important to people than your knowledge."

* * *

A small shop-front building on Simmonds Street housed the first European Church of the Nazarene in downtown Johannesburg. M. K. Fran Courtney-Smith was a student nurse in the Transvaal Memorial Hospital, and she loved that little church.

The pastor was Rev. Floyd Perkins. He and his family made the trip every weekend from Potchefstroom where he was the principal of the Bible college. It was always a special highlight when District Superintendent Dr. Strickland came to preach for them.

One morning Fran arrived for the service in her nursing uniform, ready to go on duty as soon as the service was over. She was always blessed to hear Dr. Strickland preach.

After the service Dr. Strickland shook hands with everyone at the door. Seeing Fran in uniform he said, "If you can wait a few minutes, I will give you a lift up to the nurses' home. You may still get lunch before you go on duty."

She waited and was surprised when Dr. Strickland came out wearing a white tie. He had worn the clerical collar of the English churches during the morning service. He smiled as he opened the car door and said, "I am going to an Afrikaans service tonight, and I plan to visit two dear Afrikaans folk along the way. I want them to feel comfortable with me and with our church as well."

Fran went to lunch that day wondering about the great man she had just seen drive away. Here was a man for everyone, whether English, Afrikaans, black, Coloured, Indian, or white. Here was a man who was so filled with God's love for all that he would do anything to get nearer to their hearts.

* * *

Because he communicated in their own language, Dr. Strickland's ministry was especially effective among the Afrikaans-speaking people. One Sunday morning he was preaching in one of the Afrikaans-speaking churches. He was just beginning to use the Afrikaans language, so he spoke in English. Halfway through the service, he began speaking in near-perfect Afrikaans.

An elderly couple who could not understand English at all were in that service. All of a sudden they understood, and this wonderful message struck their hearts. They both accepted the Lord as their personal Savior that morning. They later joined the church and were faithful members until their deaths some years later.

After the service one of the laymen commented to Dr. Strickland about him preaching in Afrikaans. His reply was, "Afrikaans? I didn't even know I was preaching in Afrikaans!"

* * *

One day a little Afrikaans boy held a picture card in his hand. It had an English scripture verse printed on it. As he gazed longingly at the picture, he said, "If only I could understand what it says!"

Dr. Strickland said that incident really sparked the idea and gave him the burden of printing Sunday School and other literature in the Afrikaans language.

As the new district developed, he saw the tremendous need for holiness literature in both the English and Afrikaans languages. He felt a growing conviction that Afrikaans-speaking Nazarenes needed literature in their own language. He also realized the inability of the churches to pay high prices for materials.

True to his nature, he decided to do something about it. First he mimeographed thousands of pages of Afrikaans materials. Then while the Stricklands were on furlough in the States, Bud Lunn, at the Nazarene Publishing House in Kansas City, donated a Heidelberg printing press for their work. Learning the printing procedure was the first step in providing literature for his people.

His son, Wayne Strickland, tells about this phase of his father's ministry:

"Dad liked and respected the rights of people. The first task undertaken in South Africa was to learn Afrikaans; the next was to provide literature for the church in their home language. Printed material in one's own language was high on Dad's priority list . . . high enough that I recall a printing press arriving on a truck trailer one day outside our house in Africa. The driver told Dad that he had one week to unload the press from the trailer. Thinking of it today, this press had to weigh in the neighborhood of five tons!

"Dad took the press apart piece by piece and used a wheelbarrow to move these into our garage. It took Dad more than two months to assemble it, and then more time to get the press working. From that time on the church had literature in Afrikaans. Dad stood in that garage for hours and hours every night and every Saturday."

Douglas Strickland remembers the many late nights his father spent in the garage printing and drinking black coffee to stay awake.

Missionary Herman Spencer called at their home one day. He found Dr. Strickland out in his garage printing Afrikaans literature for his people. He was dressed in overalls with ink on his hands and some smudges on his face, but he was getting literature printed. Some of his pastors thought that this was very undignified for a district superintendent, but Dr. Strickland did it willingly and gladly. Providing literature was more important to him than his dignity.

In 1963 the printing plant that had been serving the mission work of the church from its base in Swaziland united with the press operated in the garage of Dr. Strickland. A new building was erected to house this combined effort, and the Africa Nazarene Publishing House came into being in Florida near Johannesburg in South Africa.

8

I REMEMBER WHEN . . .

Charles and Fannie Strickland endeared themselves to the South African people and missionaries alike because of their warm, caring, hospitable, and generous spirit. These attributes, along with many others, contributed greatly to their outstanding leadership.

It has been many years now since the Stricklands left South Africa in 1966. However, people remember the seemingly insignificant events that had a personal touch on them and made a lasting impact on their lives.

* * *

Having English-speaking American neighbors who had such a "funny" accent was quite a novelty for Janet VanZyl. She was seven years old when the Stricklands moved in next door to her conservative Afrikaans-speaking family on Honeyball Avenue.

One year before Christmas her father and "Uncle" Strickland spent many nights testing out Buddy's new electric train set. She remembers that the engine didn't last very long once Buddy had it because the "big boys" had played with it too much before Christmas.

Janet and her mother gave their hearts to the Lord in a service where Dr. Strickland preached at the Regents Park church. Her father helped him a great deal with his Afrikaans, and her mother was his secretary for many years. The Stricklands made a great impact on Janet, and to her he was a "saint."

* * *

The cold winds were beginning to blow as winter drew near in early May on the highveld of Southern Africa in 1963. Young Leonie Alexander and her family lived on the Bible college campus where her mother was the matron and her father was a part-time lecturer. The old Bible college building was cold, and the chilly wind came whistling down the open chimneys.

Leonie had an old fireplace in her bedroom that didn't work. The only thing it did was let in the wind. She tried to find a way to close the chimney permanently. Crunching up pages of newspaper and stuffing them up into the opening seemed to be her quickest and best defense against the biting cold.

When the Strickland's oldest son, Charles, came by she felt very pleased with her accomplishment as she told him what she had done.

She was most surprised when Dr. Strickland himself came by the next afternoon and asked to see the offending fireplace. Nonplussed for a moment, Leonie thought she had done something wrong. But he told her that a useless fireplace may as well be removed and something else put in its place. After looking it over and taking measurements, he said he would take care of it.

Bright and early on Saturday morning, Dr. Strickland arrived there in his overalls and with all the tools he would need to demolish the fireplace. He began knocking it out brick by brick. Leonie protested above the noise that he really shouldn't be doing that, and she was sure she could get someone else to do it. Her protests went unheeded, so she decided to grab a wheelbarrow and haul the broken bricks away.

Leonie recalls: "I watched this great man change that dingy fireplace into a beautiful inlaid bookshelf that had a special place in my heart all the years I stayed in that room. It was always a reminder to me of a district superintendent who rubbed shoulders with important people . . . yet he took time for someone like me.

"As the years went by and he later became my father-in-law, I would always think of him when I heard Rudyard Kipling's words, 'If you can talk with crowds and keep your virtue . . . or walk with kings nor lose the common touch . . . '"

* * *

Mrs. June Alexander recalls: "Dr. Strickland was truly great in that he never bore a grudge. How well I remember one occasion on which he was so deeply hurt, our hearts ached for him. Yet, the very next week he instructed his wife to invite all the parties involved to a dinner at the district parsonage."

* * *

Missionary nurse Juanita Pate came to Johannesburg the day before she was to fly out for her first furlough in 1961. Dr. Strickland took her into town to get traveler's checks and to see the travel agent.

On arriving at the airport the next day, Dr. Strickland said he was sure her luggage was overweight. She already knew this but was prepared to pay the extra cost. He suggested that she repack before she went inside to check in. He assured her that she wouldn't wear much of what she was taking home . . . that her clothes were somewhat outdated and that she would no doubt go shopping for some new things in the States. So, there in the parking lot of the airport Dr. Strickland helped Juanita repack her cases in the trunk of the Strickland's car in order to avoid any extra cost. And how right he was!

* * *

About a year after Gideon and Jeanette Tredoux joined the Church of the Nazarene, he felt the call of God to prepare himself for full-time Christian service. They had just helped their pastor buy a car, so they did not have any money to go to Bible college.

In faith they wrote a letter to Dr. Strickland and told him about their desire to go to Bible college. He replied that there were no facilities for married couples at the college.

Later they wrote again saying that Jeanette was willing to go stay with her parents so that Gideon could do his studies. At that time they had one son and were expecting their second baby.

When Dr. Strickland received their letter and sensed their desire and circumstances, he wept before the Lord. He prayed that God would make a way for Gideon to go to Bible college because there was such a great need for pastors.

The telephone rang while he was still on his knees in his office with Gideon's letter in his hand. A young pastor informed him, "I have just received an inheritance and want to pay for a student who wants to go to college to study full-time."

Dr. Strickland cried out his reply, "I have that man. I have his letter in my hand."

Seeing the hand of God in this, he pled with the college board to open the door for the first married couple to go to live at the college. So, the Tredouxes were able to go together.

Gideon looks back: "We saw in Dr. Strickland not only a strong leader but also a man of deep compassion."

Soon after they graduated from college, Dr. Strickland asked them to pastor a church that had deep financial problems. The church would not be able to pay a pastor's salary. After much prayer, the Tredouxes felt they were to step out in faith and accept the assignment. Dr. Strickland said he would send them some money each month from his own salary. Gideon and Jeanette declined his offer, but every month an anonymous letter arrived with money in it. They always knew who sent it.

* * *

One day before bringing his message, Dr. Strickland asked the pastor, Kosie Coetzee, to read the scripture passage. As he opened his Bible a loose page fell out on to the floor. Although Dr. Strickland didn't comment at the time, the next time he came he brought the pastor a new Bible. When he gave it to him he said, "Brother Coetzee, one day you will want to read from John and then John is not there!"

* * *

While David and Myrna Whitelaw were in their first pastorate, Dr. Strickland visited them for a series of special services. Myrna was expecting their first daughter, Beverly Anne, and she was experiencing "morning, noon, and night" sickness.

Dr. Strickland noticed Myrna's condition. When he left they found a note and his own Zenith portable radio that had always accompanied him on his travels. He wanted her to enjoy it. It gave her endless hours of pleasure and relieved some tiresome and difficult days.

The Whitelaws say, "This incident was typical of the thoughtfulness and generosity of the Stricklands."

* * *

Mrs. Itha Botha was a pastor's wife in the early days of the work. She reminisces: "When our baby was dying in the Children's Hospital in Johannesburg, Dr. Strickland stayed with us from late afternoon until the next morning at five o'clock when she passed away. He was uplifting through it all.

"He was surely a great man with a tender and loving heart. He loved the Lord and served Him with all his heart."

* * *

Kosie and Hester Coetzee's son was only four months old when he had to undergo a very serious operation. It didn't look like he would survive. The Stricklands came often to the hospital during the weeks he was there and prayed with them. Dr. Strickland sent a message to all the churches asking for prayer. Kosie and Hester were deeply grateful that the Lord touched their son and healed him completely.

When it came time for the baby to be released from the hospital, Dr. Strickland drove them home, as the roads were not good and travel was difficult.

They recall, "What that meant to us is difficult to describe. We can say he was a man like Jesus, full of compassion and love."

* * *

When General Superintendent Dr. G. B. Williamson visited the work in Africa in 1961, he found that Charles was very overworked and beginning to have some physical problems due to stress. Being a keen golfer, he urged Dr. Strickland to take up golfing to give him some exercise and help him relax.

Dr. Strickland asked young missionary Norman Zurcher if he would play golf with him. In her delightful southern accent Fannie joined in, "Norman, won't you play golf with Charles? You may well save his life!" So, both men took a couple of golf lessons and on occasion they enjoyed a game of golf together.

* * *

General Superintendent and Mrs. Powers visited Africa in 1950. They were to arrive by ship in Cape Town some 900 miles from the Johannesburg area where both the Stricklands and Esselstyns lived.

Dr. Strickland and Dr. Esselstyn arranged to drive by car down to Cape Town to meet the Powers. As Dr. Strickland had not been in Cape Town up to that time, Dr. Esselstyn was driving the car as they entered the city. They were driving through the outskirts of the city when Dr. Strickland remarked, "You know, I like your driving! You don't let little things bother you!"

That made Dr. Esselstyn feel good—at first! Then Dr. Strickland told him this story:

He had been driving Dr. Powers to a meeting in Texas when, as they passed through a town, the Doctor said to him, "Charles, I like your driving! You don't let little things bother you. For example, most of us would have been troubled by the little red light back there and even stopped to look at it awhile. But you didn't let it bother you at all!"

The two men had been talking and Dr. Esselstyn had inadvertently run a red light. Dr. Strickland couldn't let the opportunity pass without telling the story on himself.

* * *

In 1955, the district had a youth camp on the banks of the Vaal River. One afternoon the young men decided to play a game of rugby. All pastors present were coaxed into playing with them. During the first half of the game, they were all duly impressed with Dr. Strickland's handling of the ball.

In the course of the evening he told his young congregation that in the game that afternoon, his head had been mistaken for the ball. This brought a good laugh from the crowd.

9

FROM THE HEART

The lives of Charles and Fannie Strickland influenced and touched a great variety of people while on their sojourn serving God and the church in southern Africa. Whether family, minister, laymen, missionaries, or nationals . . . all agree that the powerful influence of the Stricklands made a great impact on them for God and good. These testimonies and tributes will speak for themselves:

* * *

Greatness and great leadership may be defined under two headings—the tangibles and the intangibles. The intangibles are those personal characteristics for which there are no words. But they are necessary for effective leadership. To have done the task in South Africa as Dr. and Mrs. Strickland did, these intangibles were absolutely imperative.

People loved to be with him. They hung on to his words when he spoke. They waited to hear his stories and laughed with him at his jokes.

Intangibles are gifts from God. He gives them to persons whom He designates and calls to build His kingdom. But there are also tangibles. We have words to describe tangibles. Dr. Strickland had tangibles in abundance. What are they? It appears to me that they cluster in triplets: wisdom, love, mercy; compassion, loyalty, faithfulness; purpose, poise, stability; foresight, insight, and judgment.

Greatness must have focus. South African men gathered around his leadership. They listened to his exhortations, his explanations, his vision. He inspired them, envisioned them, and the church grew.

Finally, great men have a sense of humor. Dr. Strickland had it. He was also human.

One year in October, near his birthday, he was weary. My first wife and I secured tickets to hear a world-famous cellist in the great hall of the University of the Witwatersrand. The Stricklands accepted our invitation to attend with us. Since it was near his birthday I took a present along and laid it in the seat between us as we drove. The ladies were chatting in the backseat. Dr. Strickland looked down at this little package nicely tied with ribbon. I handed it to him and said, "Doc, you know you've been a little weary, and I think your sermons have been deteriorating a little. So I discovered a few days ago the latest edition of some exegetical studies on the New Testament. And I thought that this might improve your sermons."

He became very serious as he unwrapped my package and then began to laugh. We laughed all the way into the hall, because they were the four latest editions of "Peanuts."

I've been the recipient of many providential gifts and privileges and blessings in my lifetime. Among those blessings so providentially bestowed I count the privilege of close association with the Strickland family for almost a lifetime, the most precious of all mankind.

—Dr. Floyd Perkins
Nazarene Bible College, Colorado Springs
Founders Day, October 1988

* * *

Picture a man with a bush hat, khaki clothes, and a brown Ford pulling a trailer loaded with tent and chairs—planting the Church of the Nazarene among the South African Europeans, with Mom to help and four boys to hinder.

He traveled 1 million miles in Africa preaching God's Word. He took us many places. When he traveled without us, we always gave him a great welcome home and looked through his suitcase for the trinkets that he always brought his boys.

Thanks to Bud Lunn and the Heidelberg printing press, we were finally able to capture Dad at home more often. This era ended with the boys in love with Dad . . . and his Africa.

—Rev. Charles (Bud) Strickland, Jr.
Nazarene Bible College, Colorado Springs
Founders Day, October 1988

* * *

Our family was, and still is, close. Dad and Mom taught us, but above everything else, showed us what love is . . . and they lived it every day.

To us, their children, they were surprisingly liberal. We answered to God, not to them, and imposing their beliefs without knowing God was not their way. That is not to say that if the rules of the house were broken we weren't punished. I mean liberal in the sense that religion for religion's sake was not forced upon us.

The choice for our future rested within us. There was never pressure to follow in Dad's footsteps, even though one was called to the ministry, which I know delighted Dad.

Dad had an understanding of how to deal with people. He also understood that the church was composed of people with different backgrounds, cultures, and personalities. Until one understood the other's point of view, you would only see one side of the issue. I believe that simple advice and philosophy has helped this son as much as anything else Dad taught us.

Dad did not share the hurt, joy, or sorrow he dealt with daily in his ministry with me. I never knew who his favorite people were, or if so-and-so was causing problems. And for all this I grew to understand that Dad believed what he preached in all areas of his life.   —Wayne Strickland, son

* * *

I remember my father as being a deeply spiritual man who rose early and started each day with prayer and study.

64

He usually had several hours in before the rest of us got up.

—Douglas Strickland, son

* * *

Some of my fondest memories of Dad were the times we got to spend alone with him away from the business of our world. I remember a camping trip on the back of Pikes Peak in Colorado. It was at this time that he taught us about his values and beliefs, especially Christ's teaching about loving and caring for others. I learned by watching him that he applied these beliefs to everyday life. He was an exceptionally compassionate man and always took time for others regardless of their status. I feel grateful to Dad for his love and example.   —Dudley Strickland, son

* * *

It was my high privilege to first become acquainted with Dr. and Mrs. Charles Strickland when having lunch together with them in St. Louis at the 1948 General Assembly.

They arrived in South Africa later that year and from then on we worked in beautiful harmony together.

Although Dr. Strickland's mission was primarily to the white population and ours to those of other races and languages, yet in some areas there was overlapping of our work. We both sought to make the church one regardless of race, nationality, or language. We tried to be as helpful as possible to each other, always seeking God's guidance in these efforts.

The Stricklands made their home a blessing and refuge for all. Their lives were a powerful influence toward Christian unity transcending the barriers of language, nationality, and race.

He always preached with conviction and urgency, but also with tenderness, compassion, and very often with tears. He was truly a man of God who blessed and enriched the lives of all who knew him and especially those who, like myself, had the privilege of working together with him.

—Dr. W. C. Esselstyn, retired missionary
former Africa mission superintendent

I arrived in South Africa for the first time in September 1962. It was a time of many firsts for me—my first flight, my first time out of the U.S.A., my first close contact with "real, live missionaries," and I was both weary and wary.

Mrs. Strickland had prepared a tea for all the newcomers and newly returned missionaries. Their open, warm hospitality put me at ease and made me feel a part of the Africa missionary family from the very first day.

Whenever the Stricklands were out in the Eastern Transvaal for preaching and on every occasion when I was in the Johannesburg area, they always made time to find out how things were going in my life and work. Their love and prayerful concern were always evident. Every contact with them through the years exuded love and warmth.

—Rose Handloser, missionary

* * *

Arriving in Africa in 1959 as young missionaries we were privileged to get acquainted with Dr. and Mrs. Strickland. Although they had many responsibilities of their own, they always gave us their special undivided attention when we were with them. Their positive, optimistic attitude was a real inspiration to us as we started our missionary career.

We lived in the same area for several years and were privileged to have them come to speak at many of our camps, revivals, and other special meetings. They were interested in our work and concerns and were great encouragers.

Their life, marriage, and ministry was a role model for all of us who had the privilege of knowing them.

—Carol Zurcher, missionary

* * *

My first time to meet with Dr. C. Strickland was in March 1955 at Moroka Church of the Nazarene in Soweto, Johannesburg. Our relationship developed tremendously as God's children. He became a living testimony in my personal life. Despite the fact that he was white and I am black, Dr. Strickland treated me with no segregation. We were brothers. What was important to him was the fact that both of us were washed by the blood of Jesus.

I personally saw no difference between his words and works. What he said was his real life. A single thought about Dr. Strickland's life and ministry revives my life.

—Rev. J. Ndhlovu, retired district superintendent

* * *

I was the zone NYPS chairman in the late 1950s. We had a bunch of "eager beavers" on the committee and some of us had very little organizational background in the Church of the Nazarene. Dr. Strickland was serving as interim pastor of the Johannesburg church as well as district superintendent. We consulted him regarding some problems we had.

He invited us over to their home one Saturday. When we arrived, he was preparing some hamburgers and served us himself. He was dressed in relaxed sportswear and put us at ease.

After awhile he told us a story of how a car is steered around a dangerous corner. It was a very simple account, but we can recall how he put his hands on one leader's shoulders and demonstrated the way a turn could be made carefully under tricky circumstances. He did not have to suggest that a sudden, sharp tug at the wheel would be disastrous.

The idea we went away with was that he would work on some gentle, but clear, changes of direction. We, in turn, felt honor-bound to do the same.

It has stayed with me in many difficult settings since: most changes of direction should be made firmly and surely (not sharply and suddenly) toward a new objective.

—Dr. David Whitelaw, professor, Olivet Nazarene University

* * *

I always had a high esteem for this man of God. What a leader he was! He was a great American, a very good friend, a dedicated Christian, and a born leader. His life and influence on my life as a young pastor was tremendous!

I still use many of his words and thoughts. His high principles have become part and parcel of my life. The crossing of our paths has made me a better man. The crossing of his path with a multitude of South Africans led to the South African Church of the Nazarene—the salvation of lost sinners and the sanctification of God's people in this lovely country.   —Rev. L. J. Kriel, retired minister

* * *

We admired Dr. Strickland for trying to speak the Afrikaans language. He was one of the few overseas leaders who tried to learn Afrikaans and to communicate in it. This endeared him to many on the South African District. Mrs. Strickland, being a very warmhearted, friendly person was also well-loved.

We will always be grateful to God that He sent Dr. Charles Strickland to Africa. That is how we met the Church of the Nazarene and its message; how we came to live a Spirit-filled life. We also discovered, through the church, God's plan for our lives—to become missionaries.

—Rev. Jaap Kanis, missionary to Botswana

* * *

What a friend Dr. Charles Strickland was to us in South Africa! A prince among holiness preachers, a sympathetic, wise counselor, yet uncompromising.

He was always diplomatic in his approach to others whose views differed from his God-given convictions. "We're not here to fight anybody," he once said. "We're here to proclaim the doctrine of full salvation." And this he did with love and power.

What more can I say? His memory will "lie buried deep in the realms of our hearts where time stands still."

—Mrs. June Alexander, wife of retired pastor

10

TIME FOR A CHANGE

The weather was hot, humid, and unpleasant in Miami, Fla., that June in 1972. Delegates to the 18th General Assembly of the Church of the Nazarene were endeavoring to elect a general superintendent for their denomination. Having reached the church's mandatory retirement age for general superintendents, Dr. Samuel Young, who had been serving since 1948, would be stepping down upon adjournment of the General Assembly. The election process had become somewhat tense, albeit intriguing.

In some ways it had not been the happiest General Assembly. There were several reasons for this. Without question, the weather with its high humidity, as well as threatening reports of a possible hurricane forming in the Caribbean just east of Miami, contributed to a certain sense of uneasiness that pervaded the atmosphere. In addition to the meteorological threat was the conclusion many Nazarenes reached that they simply were not welcome in Miami Beach. Many felt the facilities could have been improved upon. Distance between the hotels and the convention center was great enough to border on being inconvenient. Having to scout for eating places added to the irritation.

Then there were the issues being considered; or should one say, the issues some people wanted considered. Actually, the agitators appeared to be more on the outside of the church fellowship than on the inside. Charismatic influences were beginning to infiltrate much of church life in America. There were those who seemed determined these influences would penetrate theological defenses in the Church of the Nazarene as well. As it turned out, much of the unrest was being caused by some who had formerly been members of the church, as well as a few dissidents within. Their political motives became suspect as General Assembly proceedings got underway. The literature they generously distributed as people entered the great hall did not contribute to the unity and harmony so desperately needed. To the contrary, it simply helped increase the tension sensed by all.

One of the leading churchmen seemingly destined for election as a general superintendent was suddenly plateauing in the voting process. Many had felt his election was a foregone conclusion. However, there had been rumors and innuendoes circulating about him. These had falsely placed him on the wrong side of these hidden agenda issues. Consequently this had tainted him enough in the minds of a sufficient number of delegates that election for him had reached an impasse.

A contender began to emerge who also had excellent credentials for the position. Likewise for him, however, the swing in voting was not sufficient to secure his election. Indeed, it appeared that the agitators had succeeded in doing to the Church of the Nazarene, via the issue they so passionately promoted, what the charismatic movement had succeeded in doing historically to a number of church fellowships. Would the General Assembly of the Church of the Nazarene now also be hopelessly divided?

The victims of the dilemma were innocent enough, and both of them emerged as the great churchmen they were. One of them went on to be elected general superintendent by a strong vote, four years later. He was the one who had been falsely maligned by the rumors and innuendos. The other became one of the church's strongest and ablest district superintendents. But the Miami General Assembly had to have been a most unpleasant time for both of them as well as for the delegates who could not reach agreement.

Sitting in the section reserved for the official delegation was the president of Nazarene Bible College in Colorado Springs, Colo., Dr. Charles Strickland. He had been serving in this capacity a little less than eight years. He had been requested to be that institution's founding president following the 1964 General Assembly. Now at this General Assembly he was one among many who had received some consideration for the general superintendency. Actually, on the first ballot there were a total of 51 who received one or more votes; on that ballot 32 delegates had written down the name "Charles Strickland." On the second ballot, however, he received only 15 votes. While 32 represented a fairly significant number of supporters, it was hardly enough to arouse his own interest in the possibility of being elected. He knew that one would have to receive approximately 430 votes in order to be elected. Besides, his own sense of humility would not allow him to even consider such as a possibility. On ballot No. 3 he dropped down to 1 vote, and for the rest of that Tuesday of the General Assembly, he received no votes for consideration for this office.

This refusal to be ambitious for position had already been demonstrated in Portland, Oreg., at the 1964 General Assembly. Those present on that occasion will never forget the debate that took place regarding the establishment of Nazarene Bible College. That debate just may be considered an ecclesiastical landmark by future historians of the Church of the Nazarene. Charles Strickland had been one of those who listened keenly to the arguments presented on both sides of the issue. When the vote was finally taken he cast his lot with those who favored starting a Bible college. He later observed that he did so with a certain distant interest. It didn't make that much difference to him personally one way or the other. He had served in Africa, and to Africa he would return. In fact, after the debate was over and the decision to establish a school had been made, Charles casually commented to his wife, "I sure pity the person who has to take that assignment."

The rest of the story is now history. He turned out to be that person. Under his leadership the school not only had been established but also had proven to be a successful venture. By 1972, the school had captured the imagination of the denomination. Its validity was fully recognized and acknowledged. No one would question that Charles Strickland deserved the confidence of those 32 people who had voted for him on the first ballot.

The voting had now gone into the fourth day of the General Assembly. It was Wednesday, June 21. The balloting continued to reveal that Charles Strickland really wasn't being considered a serious contender for the office of general superintendent. As a matter of fact, on the eight, ninth, and tenth ballots cast this fourth day the records show Charles Strickland never received more than two votes on any one ballot.

Awakening Wednesday morning in their hotel room, Charles found that his wife was not feeling well due to the heat and humidity of Miami Beach. A severe sinus headache convinced Fannie to remain in her room at least until later in the morning. They agreed to meet at noon for lunch. Later, when she began to feel better, Fannie got up and prepared to meet Charles.

The morning business meeting was still in session. She slipped into the proceedings and took a seat that had been reserved for her by her brother and his wife. She was greeted by her brother asking rather sharply, "Where have you been?"

She gave a quick explanation and then proceeded to raise questions of her own. "Who did they elect?" she asked.

"No one."

"You mean they haven't elected either of the two front runners?" she inquired further.

"Neither one."

"Well," asked Fannie, "who are they voting on now?"

"Charles."

"Charles? Charles who?" responded Fannie quite innocently.

On ballot No. 11 he had received 8 votes and on ballot No. 12, 23 had voted for him. It still wasn't as many as he had received on the very first ballot. But on ballot No. 13 it was noted that 127 had now cast their votes for him, and on ballot No. 14, 319 had done so. It was at this point Fannie had arrived and begun to question her brother.

By this time others sitting around Fannie became aware of her questions. There were some people sitting directly in front of her who heard the entire conversation. They burst into laughter as her brother had to explain to her that it was her husband, Charles, who was about to be elected. She was not easy to convince.

But then it happened very quickly. The board of tellers returned with their tally of votes for ballot No. 15. There were 641 ballots cast. It would take 428 votes to elect. The results were read. Charles Strickland had received 483 votes. Quick reading of the remainder of the ballot resulted in Chairman Dr. Edward Lawlor's declaring Charles Strickland duly elected as the 22nd general superintendent of the Church of the Nazarene.

All of this had taken place just after Fannie Strickland's arrival in the auditorium. In recounting this event she has simply observed: "That was a shock!" Indeed it was a shock for Charles as well. Immediately he was called to the platform. The fact that his election was so unanticipated, coupled with Charles' own natural sense of humility, made the occasion a very memorable and moving moment.

After the brief presentation, General Superintendent Strickland started to return to his seat among the delegates where he had been sitting. It was quickly explained to him that he was expected to remain on the platform where a seat was reserved for him as a general superintendent. He dutifully responded. He really preferred to be with Fannie. He needed to talk to her, and he knew she needed to talk to him as well. All of this would seem such a disruption of life's routine for them. But now a servant of the general church, time alone with his wife would have to wait until the noon adjournment. He would have to be patient, and so would she. Events of importance in their lives were always shared with one another. This exciting and unanticipated event would require a special entry in the safari journal. But it would be at least a little while before they could record it and reflect on it.

Unfortunately, the luncheon date didn't offer the two of them opportunity to be alone. Now came the flood of congratulations. Not only did many come to offer their prayers and best wishes, but some came to introduce themselves and explain how it was that they were especially significant in bringing about his election. It will be remembered that several ballots of the day before had left Charles with only one vote. This at the time had prompted Fannie to tease her husband: "Charles, you simply must quit voting for yourself," she said. Of course, as far as Charles was concerned, voting for himself was unthinkable. He always insisted, however, that at least six or eight delegates declared themselves to have cast the one lone ballot for him that had kept his candidacy alive.

When the time came for the special service of installation in front of the large assembled body, Fannie joined Charles.

General Superintendent George Coulter read the charge as follows:

> We welcome you, Charles H. Strickland, to the Board of General Superintendents of the Church of the Nazarene —to its fellowship, its privileges, its responsibilities, and its demands.
>
> The 18th General Assembly has honored you by electing you to this high office. It has expressed its confidence in you as a man of God and as a spiritual leader. Through the voice of the church we trust you have heard God's voice.

We believe that within the inner recesses of your heart is a willing acceptance of His will and purpose for the course you now assume.

The Board of General Superintendents consists of six members. You are now coequal with your colleagues. Your judgment, your involvement, and your contribution in the council chambers and throughout the church are not only desirable but necessary. Final judgments of the board must have the full support of all the members. You will be expected to contribute to the unity and strength of the board by your creative contributions of mind and spirit. No man succeeds another on this board. Your place is distinctly your own under God and by the will of the people.

The Church of the Nazarene expects leadership from those who serve in this high office. She will support those who dare to lead regardless of the personal costs involved. You must defend and proclaim the doctrines and standards which the church holds dear. Your course cannot be one of independence, but one of mutual trust and confidence with your brethren. You will be expected to promote the great worldwide enterprises of the church with all the strength and influence at your command. You must guard against the intrusion of any attitude, program, or activity into the life of the church that will weaken her spiritual fiber and dissipate her effectiveness. You will be welcomed by our people as you lift your voice in the proclamation of our central message of heart holiness.

The glamour of an election will soon fade as you assume the burdens and duties that will be laid upon you. Of necessity you will become a traveler. Your days at home and your times for rest and relaxation will be seriously curtailed. You will be absent from loved ones and family for long periods. In many lonely places you will wrestle with problems and labor to find solutions. You will become the servant of others and of the church. The cares of the church will be upon you constantly.

But we remind you that the battle is not ours but the Lord's. We admonish you to lean on the promises of God's divine grace, for He has promised, "My grace is sufficient for thee." We offer you the love, confidence, and prayers of the members of the Board of General Superintendents. We offer you the affection and loyalty of half a million Nazarenes who will take you to their hearts and call your name daily at the throne of grace. Be strong and very courageous! Endure hardship as a good soldier of Jesus Christ. "Stir up the gift of God." "That good thing which was committed unto thee kept by the Holy Ghost which dwelleth in us." "Preach the word; be constant in season, out of season; reprove, rebuke, exhort with all longsuffering and doctrine." "And the Lord shall deliver you from every evil work, and will preserve you unto his heavenly kingdom: to whom be glory for ever and ever. Amen."

Upon adjournment of the General Assembly of the Church of the Nazarene, Charles Henry Strickland became the 22nd general superintendent of his denomination.

11

KANSAS CITY— HERE WE COME

It would take some time before the reality of what took place in Miami would sink in. Those closest to Charles Strickland would frequently speak of his transparent nature. He really was devoid of any ecclesiastical ambition. Understandably, he was shaken over it all. But it did happen, and it was true; Charles H. Strickland was now a general superintendent of the Church of the Nazarene.

The Strickland family had, of course, been used to making adjustments. At the time of his election they were living in Colorado Springs. After 18 years of service in Africa, Charles had been elected president of the proposed new Nazarene Bible College. This assignment also was one that this man had hardly envisioned for himself.

True, he had felt his Africa assignment was coming to an end. He had accomplished all he had set out to do and then some. It was true he felt the time had come for new leadership for the now flourishing European District. A position had been offered him at Olivet Nazarene College in Kankakee, Ill. He considered the offer seriously and planned to accept when a call from General Superintendent Powers again altered his course of action.

This time Dr. Powers said he had been meeting with the newly elected board of the planned Bible college to be located in Colorado Springs. This board wanted Charles to be the president. During the 18 years he had spent in South Africa, the work had grown from nothing to 23 churches and 911 members.

The fact that Dr. Powers had called Charles to tell him of the vote of the board was significant in itself. It was confirmation to the Stricklands that he agreed to the timing of their return to the United States. But there was more.

The 1964 General Assembly of the church held in Portland, Oreg., has been mentioned already. It was also a historic event of sorts. The Stricklands, along with thousands of other Nazarenes, had been fascinated with the debate between members of the Board of General Superintendents relative to the establishment of a Bible college. Attention had zeroed in on two general superintendents in particular. They were Dr. Hugh C. Benner and Dr. G. B. Williamson. One was for the Bible college and one was against. This debate is reviewed historically by many in the church as a rather healthy exercise at which time two skilled speakers presented two sides of the issue in such precise language as to enable the delegates to make a clear-cut choice. The final decision was in favor of the new college.

All of the above created a dilemma for the Stricklands. As already stated, at the time of the debate Charles made the comment to Fannie that he certainly pitied the person who would be selected to establish the college. Now that he was that person, there arose another unique problem for the new president and his wife.

Following the General Assembly in 1964, the Stricklands had returned to Africa and were still there when Dr. Powers called him about the college. The problem lay in the fact that Dr. Benner had just been given jurisdiction for Africa. He and his wife would be visiting the field before the Stricklands left for America. Dr. Benner had been very outspoken in his opposition to the establishment of a Bible college. Now he would be coming out to visit the very man who was to be the institution's first president.

By now Dr. Strickland had accepted the election. Both Charles and Fannie faced this encounter with anxiety.

Their fears, however, were without foundation. No sooner had the Benners arrived but they offered their obviously very sincere congratulations to the new president and his wife. Furthermore, Dr. Benner told Charles that once the decision was made he not only supported the action the church had taken but had made Charles Strickland his personal choice for the new task. The general superintendent then informed him that he was appointing Rev. Milton Parrish as his successor in Africa. All of these actions became confirmation for the Stricklands that the timing for them to return to America had indeed been directed by God. These affirmations from the Benners continued over the next several years. This became very meaningful to the Stricklands.

After Charles was elected general superintendent, he and Fannie decided to move to the Kansas City area. Dr. Benner, now retired, and his wife had continued to make Kansas City their home. It was Mrs. Benner who came forward and offered her time and assistance in finding a home for Fannie and Charles.

There were others prepared to help in the move to Kansas City. Dr. Curt Smith, the former pastor friend back in Dallas days, had become the founding president of Mid-America Nazarene College at approximately the same time Charles had become president of the Bible college. Curt and Marge Smith were ecstatic that their friends would be coming to their area.

Prior to the general superintendency assignment, life in Colorado Springs had been full with many satisfying experiences. The college had acquired 105 acres of land. They deeded 4 acres over to Colorado Springs First Church and proceeded to lay out a campus plan. The first classroom building was ready in January of 1968. Two other buildings were completed shortly thereafter.

When the first class of 118 students arrived, Charles had put together a faculty, prepared a catalog, and established a library of 2,500 volumes. Because many of the students were married, 118 enrollers multiplied out into approximately 500 people, including spouses and children. This required a great deal of time and effort in finding adequate housing for everyone.

The visionary Charles Strickland projected to the board of trustees a school of up to 500 students. In his last report to the trustees before his election as general superintendent he stated that the student body totaled 486 with a full-time faculty of nine and six part-time. Buildings, land, and equipment were valued at $1,340,956. The library possessed 18,000 volumes. Furthermore, during this period the school had received full accreditation by the American Association of Bible Colleges. After his retirement from the general superintendency, Dr. G. B. Williamson, along with his wife, Audrey, joined the faculty. The ministry they had as teachers at the college was very well received.

Colorado Springs had been another exciting chapter in the journal of record on the Strickland safari. Experience alone had seemingly imminently qualified this man for the new role he was to fill. Surely the credentials attributed to him now as educator, along with those as pastor, evangelist, and pioneer superintendent, would serve him well as general superintendent.

12

WAKING UP IN GLORY

The 22nd general superintendent of the Church of the Nazarene entered into his new work with characteristic Strickland enthusiasm. Initially he saw himself as a learner. Perhaps he was awed in the presence of his new colleagues. They were indeed giants in spiritual leadership. Sitting at the board table with V. H. Lewis, George Coulter, Edward Lawlor, Eugene Stowe, and Orville Jenkins was an overwhelming experience. Or perhaps, as he frequently expressed, he did feel obligated to learn all there was to learn before active participation in important decision making. He gave himself a full quadrennium in which to learn his new job; he voted on important issues but left the debating to others.

He graduated from this self-imposed discipline immediately following the General Assembly of 1976 and his reelection. From then on he participated actively in the discussions as well as in the voting. But in many ways his contributions were of a spiritual nature. Whenever he was asked to lead in a period of devotion it always became a special time of spiritual fellowship for the board. His prayers were more often than not punctuated with tears that flowed out of a heart of love and compassion for his church.

Charles Strickland frequently fulfilled a pastoral role for his colleagues. He could sense when one of his brethren was facing a difficult situation, be it personal or something in the church. He had kind words of understanding, always given with the promise of his support and prayer. There was a special comfort knowing that this man of God was praying just for you.

During his last months in office members of the board became acutely aware of Dr. Strickland's deteriorating physical condition. Now prayers were being offered for him. Then Fannie became very ill. The very thought of his wife leaving him was almost too much for him. Miraculously God spared Fannie to him. As she began to improve his joy knew no bounds. This seemed to be accompanied by a special touch on Charles himself. With renewed vigor he plunged into the assignments that were his.

Then there was a slowing down again. He took to using a cane, so badly did his hip bother him. When the board members knelt to pray, he found it necessary to remain seated. Yet the fervency of his devotion continued to manifest itself. His concern was always the church. He especially took delight in reporting on the people who had been at the altars in his services seeking to be sanctified. Against the advice of some of his colleagues he continued to accept more preaching engagements than necessary. But preaching, winning souls, and encouraging the saints was his life and calling. He committed himself to continued excellence in service.

The General Assembly had ordered a five-year period (a quinquennium) between General Assemblies from 1980 to 1985 instead of the usual four-year interval. The purpose had been to get the dates of the General Assemblies permanently changed so as not to compete with the United States political parties for convention sites. This became a significant factor, since the Nazarene general gathering is recognized as the largest convention of its kind held in the United States.

A simple change from four years to five did pose something of a problem for the general superintendents in regard to their colleague Charles Strickland. The *Manual of the*

Church of the Nazarene calls for a general superintendent to retire if the General Assembly election takes place after the superintendent has passed his 67th birthday. Under normal circumstances Dr. Strickland would have been eligible for reelection had the General Assembly taken place in 1984 under the usual quadrennial plan. The change, however, from 1984 to 1985 placed him over the age limit for reelection. It was felt that the adjustment was made not to penalize a general superintendent but rather to accommodate the church; therefore, with approval of both the Board of General Superintendents and the General Board, the General Assembly agreed to waive the rule as it related to Charles Strickland. The General Assembly proceeded to reelect Dr. Strickland with a strong vote of confidence.

As it turned out, Dr. Strickland did not complete the four-year term to which he had been elected. His death cut it short by several months.

Dr. Strickland's passing created a vacancy on the board that raised speculation among many in the church. Should he be replaced immediately with an election by district superintendents only or should the vacancy remain until the next General Assembly? A decision was made not to call an election prior to the General Assembly, and the remaining members of the Board of General Superintendents agreed to double up on assignments until June 1989. It was more than a vacancy, however; it was the loss of a friend and brother that was keenly felt by other members of the board.

Charles Strickland thoroughly enjoyed being a general superintendent; that is, most of the time he enjoyed it. He didn't like tension anywhere in the church. Least of all did he like it to exist in the Board of General Superintendents. He carried out well the tasks given to him. He took seriously his jurisdictional assignments. Heart, body, and soul went into whatever he did. He was aware of human limitations and was quick to admit it if it appeared he had erred in judgment. If after he had sincerely and prayerfully performed a given task, his judgment in handling the matter came under question, he took it very seriously; sometimes probably too seriously. On those rare occasions his humanity surfaced, and he would offer to let another member of the board take up where they might have felt he left off. He wasn't one to run away from a problem, but neither did he want to stand in the way of a solution. No wonder he was dearly loved and admired by other members of his board.

There was an easy flow to the district assemblies he conducted. His services of ordination especially were unique times of inspiration and blessing. There were many tender moments as he looked over the ordinands, especially the younger ones, and addressed them as a father might address a child. The expression "son" was one he used frequently. Free-flowing tears were his trademark whenever he preached.

Many will recall hearing Dr. Strickland using the expression "honey" in addressing someone. This was obviously his "southernness" coming through. But he could call someone "honey" and at the same time be applying stern discipline. He was always available for counsel. Never was he too busy to take time out for one who really needed to speak to him.

If a problem was particularly difficult, his counsel would be accompanied with tears of understanding. It was those tears for which he perhaps will be best remembered. He was indeed a modern-day weeping prophet. How frequently the altars would be lined with seekers as he tenderly and lovingly extended the invitation to pray.

Whatever else is to be said of Charles Strickland, it needs to be stated that first, last, and always he was a preacher of the Word. Many will recall great but simple sermons coming from the heart of this man. Hundreds of Nazarenes still remember, for example, his great preaching on the subject of holiness at the General Assembly of 1980. The Sunday evening service became a camp meeting type service as seekers responded to the message by making their way forward from all over Bartle Hall in Kansas City to pray for sanctification. Indeed, holiness was his main preaching theme.

His burden as a church leader was not just to proclaim the message itself but strongly to defend the doctrine. He was especially concerned that charismatic encroachments would result in a diluting of the cardinal emphasis of his church. He was keenly aware of the dangers in this, for it will be recalled this was a major concern at the General Assembly in which he was elected.

As president of Nazarene Bible College, Dr. Strickland exerted leadership in kind but firm ways regarding this issue. He left no one with any doubts as to what he believed in the matter. One morning at the college he was approached by those telling him of a small group of students who in their own prayer meetings on campus were "speaking in tongues." It was, he discovered, disrupting the college. The problem was enhanced in that these young men were looked upon as being good students.

He called them into his office to discuss the matter with them. After a brief conversation with them, he determined that the reports were true. He later testified to praying quietly in quest of a strategy on how best to deal with the problem. He expressed to the young men his deepest respect for their lives as well as their Christian witness at the college. He pointed out his church's interpretation of the Scripture at this point and reminded them of the personal frustrations they would experience if they remained in the Church of the Nazarene.

But then the noble heart of the great man found a redemptive solution to the dilemma. After receiving their approval to do so, he personally called the president of another Bible college where they could feel free to continue in this practice. He gave a strong recommendation for the students to be accepted by the other college. These three young men did leave, but they did so with deep respect for

President Strickland. They continued contact with him for a number of years afterward.

It was this kind of firm yet redemptive leadership style that enhanced Dr. Strickland's effectiveness as a general superintendent. This made his superintendency especially worthwhile during some unsettling days as the denomination faced some of these problems and is without question one reason why the church has survived a somewhat difficult period. In many ways the firm but kind leadership style has resulted in an even stronger church as far as basic commitment to doctrine is concerned.

Charles Strickland returned to his home in Olathe, Kans., from a preaching assignment in Minnesota on August 8, 1988. Those who were with him there observed he was having a difficult time physically. He appeared to be terribly weary. Yet when he arrived home he chose to take care of his lawn. Fannie was in Oklahoma City at the time helping out in the home of one of their sons whose wife was expecting a baby. Charles should never have gone out and climbed on his mower that August evening. The record shows that particular day was the hottest day of that year in the greater Kansas City area. Yet mowing the lawn was relaxation for him, and he proceeded to do it all that evening.

He did not feel particularly well afterward, but after talking to Fannie on the telephone he felt better and retired for the night. Early the next morning he had severe chest pains and recognized he needed help. He called for the medics to come and then went to the door to unlock it and let them in. They immediately recognized the seriousness of the situation and took him to Olathe Medical Center. They knew there that he needed more technical care than they would be able to give. Within minutes they had Dr. Strickland in a helicopter used for medical evacuation, which took him to St. Luke's Hospital in Kansas City. Again within minutes, he was on the surgical table whereupon they found he had an aneurism in his heart that had burst. In spite of every diligent effort put forth, they could not save his life.

Much to Fannie's dismay, although she hurried back to Kansas City by airplane, she did not get to see her husband before he passed away. What remarkable years God had given them together.

Charles Henry Strickland, Jr., left a great legacy to his church. It is a legacy of commitment and service that will inspire many for generations to come. While he loved his church, his basic love was for the great Head of the Church, Jesus Christ. His deep and intense feelings of devotion to Christ were beautifully verbalized in the last editorial he wrote for the *Herald of Holiness*. He titled it "The Tie That Binds" and wrote as follows:

> I was privileged recently to be a worshiper in a beautiful service in one of our large churches. We were led by a godly pastor, a committed minister of music, and a dedicated choir into a pleasant and meaningful hour of spiritual worship. Everyone seemed to feel the uplifting presence of the Holy Spirit. The congregation was large and represented a wide and diverse composite of the community. Yet we sensed a unity and family togetherness throughout the service.
>
> The church had a large financial need. Response to the minister's appeal was unusual. Long after my departure from that service I meditated on the question: What really binds a group of people into such a fellowship and creates such a response?
>
> Of course, tradition is involved. Many of us have been raised in the "Nazarene tradition" and respond accordingly. However, many of these people who gave so freely are new Nazarenes who have come from a totally different tradition and in some cases with none at all.
>
> Doctrine is also involved. The great rallying crusade of the church has been the proclamation of our cardinal doctrine of entire sanctification around which we feel a call of destiny and upon which we justify our existence. Yet I am forced to realize that many worshiped with me today who have no

strong theological concepts; nor have all received the second crisis experience.

The covenant of membership creates a loyalty in many. We stand at the altar and covenant with God and the church to uphold the standards and give loyal support. In our day, however, covenants have been less binding than in other days.

I conclude there is a stronger cord that binds us together in worship and service. It came as a member of the choir sang "Jesus Is All I Need." Christ is the center of our worship—the tie that binds us together, the source of our fellowship and peace. May the presence of the living Christ be the center of our worship, praise, and adoration. May our prayer be, "O God, may our love and devotion to Thee produce a unity of spirit and bind us together into common purpose and goals as a church."